Diwali

THIS EDITION
Produced for DK by WonderLab Group LLC
Jennifer Emmett, Erica Green, Kate Hale, *Founders*

Editor Maya Myers; **Photography Editor** Nicole DiMella; **Managing Editor** Rachel Houghton;
Designers Project Design Company; **Researcher** Michelle Harris; **Copy Editor** Lori Merritt;
Indexer Connie Binder; **Proofreader** Susan K. Hom; **Series Reading Specialist** Dr. Jennifer Albro;
Sensitivity Reader Ebonye Gussine Wilkins, Archana Sethia,
Aasha (DK India's Diversity, Equity and Inclusion team)

First American Edition, 2025
Published in the United States by DK Publishing, a division of Penguin Random House LLC
1745 Broadway, 20th Floor, New York, NY 10019

Copyright © 2025 Dorling Kindersley Limited
25 26 27 28 29 10 9 8 7 6 5 4 3 2 1
001–349522–Sep/2025

All rights reserved.
Without limiting the rights under the copyright reserved above, no part of this publication may be reproduced, stored in or introduced into a retrieval system, or transmitted, in any form, or by any means (electronic, mechanical, photocopying, recording, or otherwise), without the prior written permission of the copyright owner.

DK values and supports copyright. Thank you for respecting intellectual property laws by not reproducing, scanning or distributing any part of this publication by any means without permission. By purchasing an authorised edition, you are supporting writers and artists and enabling DK to continue to publish books that inform and inspire readers. No part of this publication may be used or reproduced in any manner for the purpose of training artificial intelligence technologies or systems. In accordance with Article 4(3) of the DSM Directive 2019/790, DK expressly reserves this work from the text and data mining exception.

Published in Great Britain by Dorling Kindersley Limited

A catalog record for this book is available from the Library of Congress.
HC ISBN: 979-8-2171-2538-8
PB ISBN: 979-8-2171-2537-1

DK books are available at special discounts when purchased in bulk for sales promotions, premiums, fund-raising, or educational use.
For details, contact:
DK Publishing Special Markets, 1745 Broadway, 20th Floor, New York, NY 10019
SpecialSales@dk.com

Printed and bound in China
Super Readers Lexile® levels 500L to 610L
Lexile® is the registered trademark of MetaMetrics, Inc. Copyright © 2024 MetaMetrics, Inc. All rights reserved.

The publisher would like to thank the following for their kind permission to reproduce their images:
a=above; c=center; b=below; l=left; r=right; t=top; b/g=background
Alamy Stock Photo: Viren Desai 9tl, Jonathan Goldberg 21tr, Creative Touch Imaging Ltd. 11bl, NurPhoto SRL / Narayan Maharjan 26, The Protected Art Archive 12, ZUMA Press, Inc. 8; **Dreamstime.com:** Rohit Kamboj 4-5, Wong Yu Liang 7tr, Tanusree Mitra 22, Nikhil Patil 17tr, Ricky Soni Creations 14br, Ricky Soni Creations 30, Yurasova 27tr; **Getty Images:** Houston Chronicle / Hearst Newspapers / Raquel Natalicchio 9crb, Photodisc / ImagesBazaar 16, Universal Images Group / Sepia Times 11t; **Getty Images / iStock:** 18, AFP / Narinder Nanu 25tr, Amita Bajaj 7br, E+ / Rvimages 20, E+ / Triloks 3, E+ / Triloks 14bl, Naveen0301 13cr, Phive2015 1, Saiko3p 6, Subodhsathe 23br, Triloks 13bl, Triloks 19c, Abhishek Vyas 21b; **Shutterstock.com:** Abir Roy Barman 19tr, Akanksha Bhaduaria 29tl, Priya Darshan 27cr, Mila Supinskaya Glashchenko 24, Ami Parikh 29b, PhotoGullak 23tl, PradeepGaurs 17bl, Prasannapix 15, Reddees 10, Sumit Saraswat 25bl, StockImageFactory.com 28, Irina Thalhammer 7bl

Cover images: *Front:* **Dreamstime.com:** Pikepicture c/ (Lamps), Stock Image Factory b;
Getty Images / iStock: E+ / Shylendrahoode c, Girafchik123 tl, tr, Nataliia Nesterenko (Background);
Back: **Dreamstime.com:** Pikepicture cra; **Getty Images / iStock:** Lattesmile clb

www.dk.com

This book was made with Forest Stewardship Council™ certified paper – one small step in DK's commitment to a sustainable future.
Learn more at www.dk.com/uk/information/sustainability

Level 2

Diwali

Sita Jit

Contents

6	Happy Diwali!
8	Row of Lights
10	Roots of Diwali
14	Celebrating Light
24	Diwali Around the World
30	Glossary
31	Index
32	Quiz

BAPS Shri Swaminarayan Mandir, Lilburn, Georgia, US

Happy Diwali!

It's Diwali [dee-WAH-lee]! In the bustling markets and streets of India, family and friends greet each other with excitement. "Happy Diwali!" they say.

A diya [DEE-yah] flickers. Lights twinkle against the night sky. The festival of lights is here!

diya

Diwali is an exciting festival. It is important for Hindus and others in India and around the world. It is a time to celebrate with feasting, family, and fun!

Row of Lights

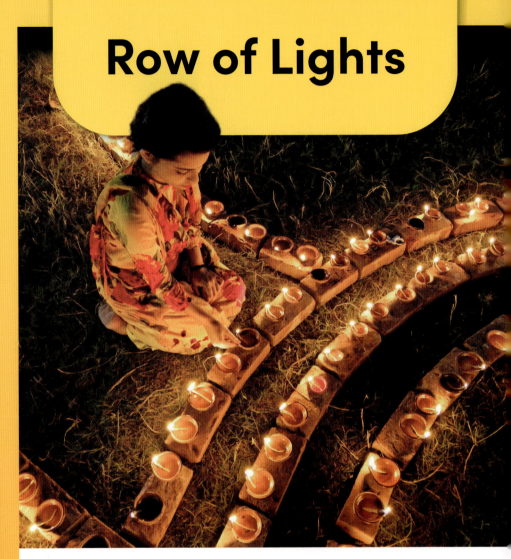

The word Diwali comes from the Sanskrit word "deepavali." Deepavali means "row of lights." So, Diwali is also known as Deepavali.

Diwali is celebrated in October or November. The date falls in the Kartika month of the Hindu calendar. This lunisolar calendar is based on positions of the sun and the moon. Diwali is celebrated on the night of the new moon.

Diwali Everywhere

Diwali is celebrated by over a billion people in India. People in the Indian diaspora also celebrate Diwali. The Indian diaspora is a worldwide community. People in the diaspora live in other countries. But they can trace their origins to India. Many other people around the world celebrate Diwali, too.

Roots of Diwali

Diwali has been celebrated for more than 2,500 years. It began as a harvest festival. Farmers gave thanks to Goddess Lakshmi for their crops. People left their doors and windows open. They lit up their homes to welcome Lakshmi in.

Now, Diwali is one of the biggest and brightest festivals of the year.

Illustration of an 18th-century Diwali celebration

Hinduism

Hinduism is one of the oldest religions in the world. Many people in India are Hindu. Hindus believe in hundreds of gods and goddesses. Lakshmi is the goddess of prosperity and wealth.

Left to right: Ravana, Rama, Lakshmana

On Diwali, many people also celebrate the story of Prince Rama. Rama was supposed to be king. But he was exiled from his kingdom. His wife, Sita, and his brother, Lakshmana, joined him in exile. Then, a king named Ravana kidnapped Sita. Rama helped to defeat Ravana.

He rescued Sita. After 14 years, they returned to Rama's kingdom. The people of the kingdom lit thousands of lamps to welcome him home. The lamps represented the end of darkness. People today light their homes to honor this story.

Rama

Celebrating Light

Diwali is a bright, colorful celebration.

People wear their finest clothes. Houses are cleaned. People decorate with twinkling lights. Relatives visit each other. Mithai [MIT-hi], or sweets, are essential to any celebration! Playing cards and exchanging gifts are also part of the fun.

mithai

Some people celebrate Diwali for one festive day, especially outside India. In India, many people celebrate smaller festivals over five days. Each day has different traditions.

The celebrations begin with a festival called Dhanteras [DAHN-teh-ruz]. People clean their homes. They believe Goddess Lakshmi will bring good fortune only to clean homes.

People also shop for new clothes. Women and girls get colorful saris, salwar kameez, or lehengas. Men buy kurtas—long, loose-fitting shirts.

kurta

This is considered a good day to buy metals like gold and silver. People buy things like jewelry and kitchen utensils. These are said to bring good luck.

Day two is called Chhoti Diwali [CHOH-tee dee-WAH-lee]. It's time to make rangoli [run-GO-lee]. People use colored powder, rice, or flower petals. They make beautiful designs on the ground. These may be at the entrance of their home or on the floor inside. The colorful art welcomes guests. It brings good luck, too!

Beautiful Patterns

Rangoli has different names in different regions of India. It is known as kolam [KO-lum] in Tamil Nadu. It is called muggu [moo-goo] in Andhra Pradesh.

People visit each other's homes. They exchange gifts and enjoy tasty mithai.

Diwali takes place on day three. This is the darkest night of the month. The moon is new. The day is packed with fun. Relatives visit with each other. They feast on delicious food. Homes are lit with diyas.

Puja [POO-jah] is an act of prayer. At home, Goddess Lakshmi is worshipped in a puja. Some people go to a mandir [MUN-dher] for blessings. A mandir is a Hindu place of worship.

Bang! Pop! Boom! In some places, the day ends with colorful fireworks!

21

The celebrations of the fourth day vary by region. In Gujarat, this day brings in the new year. Relatives wish each other a good year ahead. In other regions, Govardhan Puja [go-VAR-dan POO-jah] is performed. People cook special food. They give thanks to Lord Krishna.

People preparing food offerings for Govardhan Puja, Kolkata, India

Tilak

Sisters often place a red mark on their brothers' foreheads. The mark is called a tilak. This symbolizes love between the siblings.

The final day is called Bhai Dooj [by DOOJ]. This day is a celebration of love between brothers and sisters. Siblings exchange gifts. They share words of love and good wishes.

Diwali Around the World

Diwali is celebrated by Hindus around the world. Families take time off from work and school. Some go to the mandir together. Some have a puja at home. They feast with family and friends. Sparklers and fireworks may end the night of fun and celebration!

Diwali is an important celebration for other faiths, too.

Sikhs celebrate this day as Bandi Chhor Divas [BAHN-dee CHORE DIV-us]. Sikhs remember their religious teacher, Guru Hargobind Singh Ji. He stood up for people to be treated fairly. Now, people celebrate by lighting up their homes. They eat a special meal. They enjoy fireworks, too.

Amritsar, India

Sikhism

Sikhism began in the late 15th century. Sikhs believe in one god who created the world. They believe people should treat everyone equally. They believe people should take care of one another.

Some Buddhists celebrate Diwali. They light lamps, decorate temples, and worship the Buddha. They remember the Hindu emperor Ashoka. Ashoka was a warrior who gave up violence. He converted to Buddhism.

Kathmandu, Nepal

Statue of Buddha

Buddhism and Jainism

Buddhism is one of the world's major religions. Buddhists believe that human life is a cycle of birth and death. The cycle includes suffering. They believe it is possible to escape this cycle by reaching enlightenment. Jainism is an ancient religion. It teaches compassion for all living things. Jains are vegetarians.

Jains celebrate Diwali, too. They honor Lord Mahavira's finding enlightenment. Enlightenment is a peaceful state of being. People in the community fast. This means they go without eating or drinking at certain times. They sing songs. They meditate together.

All these stories of Diwali have something in common. Good triumphs over evil. Goodness and light are within each of us. Diwali is a special time to celebrate our light.

Lights On

Look for a home decorated with lots of lights. They may be celebrating Diwali!

No matter how it is celebrated, the festival of lights is a joyous time for all.

Happy Diwali!

Glossary

Diaspora
People settled far from the place where their ancestors lived

Diwali
A festival of lights celebrated in India and around the world

Diya
An oil lamp made of clay

Enlightenment
A state of being without suffering or desire

Fast
To not eat or drink during a certain period

Kartika
The eighth month in the lunisolar Hindu calendar

Lunisolar
Relating to both the sun and moon

Mandir
A temple or place of worship

Meditate
To think deeply or reflect either in silence or with chanting

Mithai
Indian sweets

Puja
An act of prayer that involves rituals

Rangoli
Intricate designs, usually made at the entrance of a home from colored rice flour or powder

Tilak
A sacred red mark placed on the forehead

Index

Buddhists 26–27
clean homes 16
clothes 14, 17
diaspora 9
diya 7, 20
enlightenment 27
fast 27
gifts 14, 19, 23

goodness 28
Hindus 7, 11, 21, 24
Jains 27
Kartika 9
Lakshmi (goddess) 10, 11, 16, 21
lunisolar calendar 9
mandir 21, 24

mithai 14, 19
puja 21, 24
Rama, Prince 12–13
rangoli 18–19
siblings 23
Sikhs 25
tilak 23

Quiz

Answer the questions to see what you have learned. Check your answers in the key below.

1. When is Diwali celebrated?
2. What are the small oil lamps lit on Diwali called?
3. What is a rangoli?
4. True or False: Most people in India are Hindu.
5. In addition to Hinduism, name three other religions that may celebrate Diwali.

1. October or November 2. Diya 3. A colorful patterns on the ground or floor 4. True 5. Sikhism, Buddhism, Jainism